IV

IV Publishing
Email: sales@islamicvillage.co.uk | Website: www.islamicvillage.co.uk

Distributed by HUbooks
Email: info@hubooks.com | Website: www.hubooks.com

Title: Selected Prayers Upon The Prophet ﷺ
Original Author: Habib Muhammad bin ʿAlawi al-ʿAydarus
Translated by: Imran Rahim

First Edition | ISBN: 978-0-9520853-5-5

Typesetting and Cover Design Concept
Etherea Design | enquiries@ethereadesign.com

OUTSTANDING

Printed & bound in the United Kingdom by OUTSTANDING
Email: books@outstanding-media.co.uk Tel: +44 (0)121 327 3277

SELECTED PRAYERS *upon* THE PROPHET

صلى الله عليه وسلم

HABIB MUHAMMAD
BIN ʿALAWI AL-ʿAYDARUS

It is reported on the authority of Ubayy b. Kaʿb that he said,

> *'O Messenger of God, I wish to send abundant prayers upon you, so how much of my prayers should I dedicate to you?'*
>
> *So he ﷺ said, 'As much as you want.'*
>
> *I said, 'A quarter?'*
>
> *He ﷺ said, 'As much as you want, but were you to do more, it would be good for you.'*
>
> *I said, 'A half?'*
>
> *He ﷺ said, 'As much as you want, but were you to do more, it would be good for you.'*
>
> *I said, 'Two thirds?'*
>
> *He ﷺ said, 'As much as you want, but were you to do more, it would be good for you.'*
>
> *I said, 'Shall I then make all of my prayers for you?'*
>
> *He ﷺ said, 'Then all of your worries would be sufficed and your sins would be atoned.'*
>
> TIRMIDHI AND AHMAD

Contents

Permission to Translate

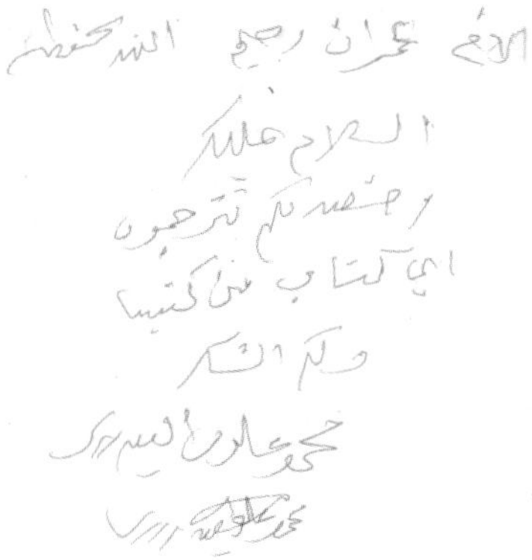
الأخ عمران رحيم الله يحفظه
السلام عليك
ويمكنكم ترجمون
اي كتاب من كتبنا
ولكم الشكر
محمد علوي العيدروس

To brother Imran Rahim, may Allah preserve you.

Peace be upon you.

You have permission to translate any of our books and we express our gratitude.

MUHAMMAD B. ʿALAWI AL ʿAYDARUS

مقدمة السلسلة السعدية

بسم الله الرحمن الرحيم

الحمد لله يسعد من يشاء بتوفيقه لطاعته وذكره وشكره وحسن عبادته وصلى الله وسلم على خير بريته وصفوته من خليقته سيدنا محمد وآله وصحبه وعترته

وبعد: فقد أبرز الله على يد شيخنا الحبيب الفاضل الكريم المنيب الخاشع المتواضع محمد سعد بن علوي بن عمر العيدروس كتابة رسائل تحتوي على فوائد وفضائل وخيرات كثيرة وقد حظى الأخ عمران رحيم بالإذن من الحبيب سعد المذكور في ترجمة رسائل وكتب إلى اللغة الإنغليزية فبارك الله له في هذا الإذن والعمل عليه لتعم الفائدة ويشارك في نشر الخير.

تقبل الله منه ووفقه وأعلى درجات الحبيب محمد سعد العيدروس وجمعنا جميعا في فردوسه الأعلى آمين

عمر بن محمد بن سالم بن حفيظ

دار المصطفى بتريم
٢٦ / ٦ / ١٤٣٤ هـ
٨ / ٥ / ٢٠١٣ م

Foreword to Series

In the name of Allah, the Beneficent, the Merciful

ALL PRAISE IS FOR ALLAH, He renders felicitous whomever He wills by granting the ability to obey Him, to remember Him, to show Him gratitude and to excel in His worship. May Allah send blessings and peace upon the best of His creation, the elect of His creation, our liege lord Muḥammad and upon his folk, his Companions and his family.

To proceed: Indeed Allah made manifest at the hands of our Shaykh, the noble and generous, the sincere, the humble and deferential Ḥabīb Muḥammad, Saʿd b. ʿAlawī b. ʿUmar al-ʿAydarūs, writings and treatise which contain numerous benefits and virtues and much good.

Brother ʿImrān Raḥīm obtained permission from the aforementioned Ḥabīb Saʿd to translate his books and treatise into the English language. May Allah bless him in his permission and in acting upon it therein in order to extend its benefit and partake in spreading its goodness.

May Allah accept this from him and grant him assistance (*tawfiq*), and may He raise the rank of Ḥabīb Muḥammad, Saʿd b. ʿAlawī al-ʿAydarūs and gather us all in His Lofty Firdaws. Āmīn!

[HABIB] ʿUMAR B. MUHAMMAD B. SALIM B. HAFIZ

Dār al-Muṣṭafā, Tarīm
26th Jumādā al Ākhira 1434 AH
7th May 2013 CE

Foreword

In the name of Allah, the Beneficent, the Merciful

ALL PRAISE IS FOR ALLAH, and may Allah send blessings and peace upon our liege lord Muḥammad ﷺ and upon his folk and Companions.

The books of our Shaykh, the gnostic, the righteous Muḥammad b. ʿAlawi al-ʿAydarūs, more commonly known as Saʿd ؓ are indeed beneficial and of immense worth. The traces of pure sincerity for the noble countenance of Allah are manifest within them.

Our blessed brother who has been granted *tawfiq* wished to extend benefit to himself and to his Muslim brethren by translating this book into the English language. He took permission from our aforementioned Shaykh ؓ during his lifetime who granted him this with his own handwriting.

We ask Allah by virtue of His favour and generosity that He accept it from us and him, and that He makes it purely for His noble countenance, and a means of benefit for the Muslims. Verily He is powerful over everything and most worthy of answering prayers.

[MUSA] KAZIM B. JAʿFAR AL-SAQQAF

Acknowledgements

I am indebted to a number of individuals without whose efforts this translation would not have been possible.

May Allah, the Generous, fill the grave of Ḥabīb Saʿd with light and raise him with the foremost, and may his works continue to manifest as gifts and divine mercy in the intermediary realm.

My gratitude extends to Sayyidī al-Ḥabīb ʿUmar b. Ḥafīẓ for writing the introduction to this series, and likewise to Ḥabīb Kāẓim al-Saqqāf for writing the foreword to this book.

This translation would not have been possible without the effort of Ustādh Amīn Buxton whose help is too extensive to mention.

I express my gratitude to Dr Javed Khan and Islamic Village Publishing for allowing this work to be published. With the same token, I would like to extend thanks to Zain ul-Abedin (Faadil) from Outstanding for his creative and technical input in producing this book. Thanks are also due to Sheikh Hāroon Ḥanīf for his assistance.

Finally, may Allah Most High bless my parents, Arif and Nasra, for their constant prayers and encouragement. May this humble work be counted from amongst their deeds.

Translator's Introduction

I thank Allah Most High for the favours He continues to bestow upon this unworthy slave, and for allowing me to undertake this attempt at serving the community of His beloved ﷺ.

This brief work focuses on a fundamental and celebrated aspect of our religion, sending *ṣalawāt* upon the Messenger of Allah ﷺ. Timeless works such as *Dalā'il al-Khayrāt* of Imām al-Jazūlī and *Qasīdat al-Burda* by Imām al-Būṣayrī have been recited in the East and the West for centuries, having been embraced by various traditions throughout the Islamic world.

This work is the first in what is hoped will be a series of translations taken from the works of Ḥabīb Muḥammad Sa'd al-'Aydarūs. Readers may already be familiar with the author, whose work *The Book of Intentions* has been published and made available to the English-speaking world. This series is an attempt to further spread the benefit of his works.

The order of this book has been changed from the original, organising the various prayers around certain themes. Footnotes have been added by the translator, unless otherwise stated. Translations of verses from the Qur'ān have been taken from The Majestic Qur'ān published by the Nawawi Foundation. An appendix has been added at the end to introduce the reader to the meaning of *ṣalawāt*, as understood by the early generations of Qur'anic commentators.

In addition to this, the transliteration for all of the prayers has been included at the end in order to facilitate reading for those unfamiliar with Arabic.

I ask Allah that He accepts this work through the door of His beloved, our Master Muḥammad ﷺ and that He brings about benefit by this work, and that it becomes a means of drawing closer for those who engage it.

Biography of Author[1]

HIS LINEAGE

He is al-Ḥabīb 'Sa'd' Muḥammad b. ʿAlawī b. ʿUmar b. ʿAydarūs b. ʿAlawī b. ʿAbdullāh b. ʿAlawi b. ʿAbdullāh b. al-Ḥasan b. ʿAlawī b. ʿAbdullāh b. Aḥmad b. Shaykh Ḥusayn b. Imām ʿAbdullāh al-ʿAydarūs b. Shaykh Abū Bakr al-Sakrān b. Shaykh ʿAbd al-Raḥmān al-Saqqāf b. Shaykh Muḥammad Mawlā al-Dawīlah, b. ʿAlī Mawlā Darak, b. ʿAlawī al-Ghuyūr, b. al-Faqīh al-Muqaddam, Muḥammad b. ʿAlī, b. Muḥammad Ṣaḥib Mirbāṭ, b. ʿAlī Khaliʿ Qasam, b. ʿAlawī, b. Muḥammad Ṣaḥib al-Sawmaʿah, b. ʿAlawī, b. ʿUbaydullāh, b. al-Imām al-Muhājir il-Allāh Aḥmad, b. ʿIsā, b. Muḥammad al-Naqīb, b. ʿAlī al-ʿUrayḍī, b. Jaʿfar al-Ṣādiq, b. Muḥammad al-Bāqir, b. ʿAlī Zayn al-ʿĀbidīn, b. Ḥusayn al-Ṣibṭ, b. ʿAlī b. Abū Ṭālib and Fāṭimah al-Zahrā', the daughter of our Master Muḥammad, the Seal of the Prophets ﷺ.

HIS LIFE

Ḥabīb Muḥammad, known by all as 'Sa'd', was born in Tarim in 1351 AH (1932 CE). He was raised, nurtured and schooled under the watchful gaze of his father,

1 This biography is taken from '*Imams of the Valley*' by Amīn Buxton published by Dar al-Turath al-Islami.

Ḥabīb ʿAlawī, one of the foremost scholars of Tarim at the time, and his pious mother, *Sharīfah* Fātima bt. Ḥasan al-Junayd. She was also the mother of two great scholars: Muḥammad and ʿAwad, sons of Ḥabīb Ḥamid b. Muḥammad Bā ʿAlawī, who were both imams of the great Masjid Bā ʿAlawī.

Ḥabīb Saʿd was assiduous in his care for his mother and later she lived with him in his house in al-Nuwaydarah until she passed away in 1410 AH (1989 CE) at the age of nearly one hundred. Ḥabīb Saʿd thus grew up in an environment of scholarship and virtuousness.

He studied under many scholars in Tarim and elsewhere. He spent six years at the Ribāṭ of Tarim under the tutelage of Ḥabīb ʿAbdullāh b. ʿUmar al-Shāṭiri. He received knowledge and spiritual guidance from Ḥabīb ʿAlawi b. ʿAbdullāh Shihāb al-Dīn and later from his son, Ḥabīb Muḥammad. Likewise, he learnt from Ḥabīb Sālim b. Hafīẓ and after him his son Ḥabīb Muḥammad. Ḥabīb ʿUmar b. ʿAlawī al-Kāf was another of his many teachers.

In 1371 AH (1951 CE), he travelled to Aden to earn a living and study at the hands of the city's scholars. In 1391 AH (1971 CE), however, he was jailed by the socialist government of the time, which in its vain attempts to suppress Islam imprisoned and killed a number of scholars. He spent three and a half years in prison enduring the most severe types of torture. Yet in spite of these circumstances, he was able to memorise the Qur'an.

After his release, he returned to Tarim in the year 1395 AH (1975 CE), where he was made the imam of the famous Masjid al-Saqqāf. The *ḥaḍra* of dhikr established in the mosque by Shaykh ʿAbd al-Raḥmān al-Saqqāf more than six hundred years previously had been suspended by the socialist authorities. However, through the efforts of Ḥabīb Saʿd, it was resumed.

In 1397 AH (1976 CE), he reopened the renowned school of Abū Murayyam for the memorisation of the Qur'an, which had been closed by the authorities. It was founded by the great Imam, Muḥammad b. ʿUmar Abū Murayyam in 822 AH (1419 CE). Thousands of great scholars have graduated from it over the centuries.

The school is known for being a place where people attain spiritual openings and a place where memorisation of the Qur'an is made easy and prayers are accepted. Ḥabīb ʿUmar b. Ḥafiẓ was one of the first students to complete his memorisation of the Qur'an after the school reopened. Ḥabīb Kādhim b. Jaʿfar al-Saqqāf also graduated at the hands of Ḥabīb Saʿd, along with many other scholars and callers to Allah. The school has since gone from strength to strength and has opened sixteen branches in and around Tarim.

In his service of sacred knowledge, he presided over a number of gatherings and lessons. One was the lesson inside the Qubbah (dome) of his ancestor, Imam ʿAbd Allāh al-ʿAydarūs, in which the *Ihyā' ʿUlūm al-Dīn* of Imam al-Ghazālī is read. He also revived the weekly reading of Ṣaḥīḥ al-Bukhārī in Masjid Bā ʿAlawī which is concluded in the month of Rajab.

Out of his desire to benefit people, he compiled over one hundred small books on numerous subjects. He believed that a book should be short, beneficial and affordable and this is how his books are. The first of them was *Kitāb al-Āyāt al-Mutashābihāt*, which assists anyone who wishes to memorise the Qur'an by mentioning verses in different parts of the Book that are either similar or the same. It was revised and published by Ḥabīb Sālim al-Shāṭiri in 1409 AH (1988 CE) and was well received by Ḥabīb ʿAbd al-Qādir al-Saqqāf.

Ḥabīb Saʿd compiled several other books on aspects of the Qur'an as well as biographies and pieces of wisdom of many of the Imams of Hadramawt. His *Kitāb al-Niyyāt* (Book of Intentions) delves deep into the science of intentions and due to its practical benefit was translated into English and several other languages. He also compiled books on subjects as diverse as remedies for forgetfulness and depression, neglected elements of the sunnah, water, mountains, cats, ants, coffee, vinegar, apples, the heart and special attributes of the number seven.

Ḥabīb Saʿd's door was always open for visitors, who came in their droves. Hardly a single visitor left without first drinking tea and being presented with his latest book. His heart was filled with mercy and compassion for all those that came to him, especially students of knowledge, whom he would assist and encourage in whatever way he could. He saw all his students as his children. He severely counseled people to respect papers on which the name of Allah or one of His Prophets was written, and not to waste food or water.

He constantly was in a state of remembrance of Allah and a substantial portion of his life was spent with the *muṣḥaf* or *masbaḥa* (prayer beads) in his hands. He would spend most of the night writing and researching, would go in the second half of the night to pray in Masjid Bā ʿAlawi and then go to Masjid al-Saqqāf to read the Qur'an with the group before Fajr.

In his final years, it was only old age and poor health that prevented him from leading the prayer in Masjid al-Saqqāf and presiding over the *ḥaḍra* and gatherings of knowledge. When he found the strength he would come, and he attended the great *khatm* of Masjid al-Saqqāf on the 21st night of Ramadan in the last year of his life, as well as the *ḥaḍra* only a few days before his death.

He often advised his students to read a portion of the *Iḥyā'* every day and it is fitting that just days before his death he was given copies of a new print of the book and he spent his last hours with this great work in his hand.

HIS DEATH

He was finally reunited with his Lord on Thursday, 8th Dhu'l-Qaʿdah 1432/6th October 2011 at the age of 82. Thousands of the people of Tarim and Hadramawt came out at ʿAsr on Friday for his funeral prayer. Before the prayer, Ḥabīb ʿUmar b. Ḥafiẓ and Ḥabīb Sālim al-Shāṭiri addressed the crowd, recounting the exploits of this great Imam and calling the people to return to Allah and hold fast to the inheritance of the their predecessors.

He was then buried in the Zanbal graveyard just outside the Qubbah of Imam al-ʿAydarūs at the top of the path which leads down to the grave of Imam al-Ḥaddād. May Allah have mercy upon Ḥabīb Saʿd and benefit it us by him.

SELECTED PRAYERS *upon* THE PROPHET

صلى الله عليه وسلم

HABIB MUHAMMAD
BIN ʿALAWI AL-ʿAYDARUS

Introduction

Know, my brother, that the sending of *ṣalawāt*[1] upon the Prophet ﷺ is from the most virtuous of acts and from the most beautiful that bequeath closeness to Allah, and whose benefits are numerous. We have gathered some such formulas in this brief work, and as we have heard from our *shuyūkh*, the sending of blessings is a guide (*shaykh*) for the one who does not have a guide, meaning that it takes the place of a *shaykh*.

We have likewise heard that at the end of times, those who nurture others (*murabbūn*) and *shuyūkh* will be few in number and nothing will remain amongst people except the sending of blessings upon the Prophet ﷺ.

So habituate yourself upon them, my brother, and have a daily litany of at least 300 and strive to be consistent upon this.

---

1 See page 75 for detail on the term *ṣalawāt*

THE INTENTION OF HABIB ABDULLAH AL-HADDAD FOR SENDING SALAWAT

O Allah, I intend by my sending blessings upon the Prophet ﷺ fulfilling Your command, and professing belief in Your book, and following the way of Your Prophet, our liege lord Muḥammad ﷺ and (declaring) love for him, yearning for him and venerating his right and to ennoble him, and he is most certainly deserving of that ﷺ, so accept this from me by virtue of Your grace and excellence.

Remove the veil of heedlessness from my heart, and make me from the righteous. O Allah, increase him in eminence through his ﷺ eminence with which You have preferred him, and increase him in honour through the honour which You have given him ﷺ, and raise his station in the stations of the Emissaries, and likewise raise his level in the levels of the Prophets.

I ask of you Your Divine pleasure and for Paradise, O Lord of Creations, with well-being in religious and worldly life and in the Hereafter.

I ask of you death upon the Book, the Prophetic Way and Community and upon the testament of faith, without change or alteration.

By Your grace and excellence towards me, forgive me for what I have sinned. Indeed you are the Oft-Returning, the Most Merciful, and may Allah send blessings upon our liege lord Muḥammad ﷺ and on his folk and his Companions.

The following is another intention from the book from which these prayers have been chosen, as an attempt to combine both of these intentions, although the intention of Imam al-Ḥaddād is better (if restricted to one), and is thus:

Verbally utter whilst bringing to one's mind and heart the meanings (*mustaḥḍiran*):

O Allah, I hereby intend to draw closer to You by sending blessings upon Your noble Prophet ﷺ as a means of worship and veneration, desiring Your pleasure and the pleasure of Your noble Prophet, intending Your Mighty Countenance alone, sincerely for Your sake alone, and it is You who favoured and preferred me by this.

At Your service O Allah, and Your good pleasure! And all good is entirely in Your hand. O Allah, bestow blessings upon our liege lord Muḥammad ﷺ and on his folk and his Companions.

VIRTUES OF SENDING SALAWAT UPON THE PROPHET[1] ﷺ

1. Fulfilling the command of Allah, Exalted be He

2. To be in accordance with the Divine act of sending *ṣalawāt* upon him ﷺ

3. To be in accordance with the angels [in sending *ṣalawāt* upon him ﷺ]

4. To embed in the heart love of him ﷺ

5. To firmly imprint his noble form within oneself, and to deeply connect to it

6. It is included in the remembrance of Allah the Exalted, and gratitude to Him, and recognising His favours upon His slave by His sending of him ﷺ

7. It is a prayer from the servant

8. Doing so is a means for the coolness of his eyes ﷺ and likewise for the one who invokes

9. The blessings of Allah will be upon the one send blessings

10. Likewise the blessings of the angels will be upon the one who send blessings

11. Attaining ten blessings from Allah, the Exalted, for the one who sends just one

12. One is raised by ten degrees

13. Ten good deeds are recorded

14. Having sins forgiven

15. It suffices the slave from worries of various afflictions

16. It takes the place of charity for the one in difficulty

17. It is purification for the invoker

18. It is a means of attaining success and achieving goals and fulfilling needs in the worldly life and in the afterlife

19. The servant becomes absolved of being termed a miser when he ﷺ is mentioned

20. It is a means for being enveloped in mercy, and how lofty a blessing that is!

21. By it, the invoker receives a response from the Prophet ﷺ

22. The invoker receives blessings in his self, his life, his actions, and it is also a means for his rectification

23. Attaining the mercy of Allah

24. One is rendered safe from the wrath of Allah, Exalted be He

25. It gives the invoker a perpetual love for the Prophet ﷺ

26. It is a means for guidance for the slave and for revitalises his heart

27. It is a means of perfuming the gathering and ensures that the attendees do not have regrets on the Day of Rising

28. It beautifies gatherings

29. To purify the heart from hypocrisy and rust

30. It necessitates people's love for the invoker, and beholding the Prophet ﷺ in the dream state and it prevents the invoker from backbiting

31. It benefits the invoker and his children and likewise his grandchildren

32. It is a means for having the name of the invoker shown to him ﷺ

33. A reward the like of Mount Uḥud is written for him

34. It corrects misdeeds and is more virtuous than freeing slaves

35. It is a means of the invoker seeing him ﷺ in a dream state

36. The invoker will see his place in Paradise before death

37. It is a means of intercession

38. It is a means of entering beneath the shade of Heavenly Throne

39. He will meet Allah whilst Allah is pleased with him

40. It helps to outweigh the Scales (when deeds are measured)

41. It is means for one arriving at the Basin (*al-Ḥawḍ*)

42. It prevents one from thirst on the Day of Rising

43. It procures safe passage on the Bridge (*al-Ṣirāṭ*)

44. It will be a light upon the Bridge

45. Numerous spouses in Paradise

46. Those who exceed in sending blessings are the most deserving of him (*awlā*) ﷺ meaning they are the closest to him on the Day of Rising

So be plentiful, my brother, in sending blessings upon him ﷺ and have a daily litany of at least three hundred. If you are in a rush or are busy then the very least is to read:

﴿إِنَّ ٱللَّهَ وَمَلَٰٓئِكَتَهُۥ يُصَلُّونَ عَلَى ٱلنَّبِيِّۚ
يَٰٓأَيُّهَا ٱلَّذِينَ ءَامَنُواْ صَلُّواْ عَلَيۡهِ وَسَلِّمُواْ تَسۡلِيمًا﴾

اللهُمَّ صَلِّ وَسَلِّمْ عَلَيهِ وَعَلَى آلِهِ

Allah and His angels bless the Prophet. O you who believe! Bless him and salute him with a worthy salutation!

O Allah, send blessings and peace upon him ﷺ and his folk.[2]

2 al-Aḥzāb (33:56)

It is best to read this in the morning and evening, using the formulas mentioned, but if not then do so with any formula.

The virtues of sending blessings on the day and night of Friday are immense and doing so in abundance is recommended due to his ﷺ saying, 'Send much blessings upon me ﷺ on the night of Friday[3] and during the day [of Friday].'

3 ie. Thursday night

اللهُمَّ صَلِّ عَلَى سَيِّدِنَا مُحَمَّدٍ وَعَلَى آلِهِ وَصَحْبِهِ وَسَلِّمْ
بِعَدَدِ كُلِّ حَرْفٍ جَرَى بِهِ الْقَلَمُ

O Allah, send blessings and peace upon our liege lord Muḥammad ﷺ and upon his folk and his Companions as many as the number of letters that flow through the pen.

Bā Sawdān says in *Meadows of the Souls*: This prayer was mentioned by the author of the book *The Object of the Seekers of Guidance in the Interpretation of Legal Verdicts by some of the Leaders from the Later Scholars* whilst he was the judge of the province of Ḥadramawt, the *Sayyid Sharīf* Abdal Raḥmān b. Muḥammad al-Mashhūr Bā ʿAlawī in *Recommended Remembrances and Supplications* from the book *Meadows of the Souls* with important additional benefits in which he said:

It is narrated from the Spiritual Axis (*quṭub*), al-Ḥaddād that reading the following after the Maghrib prayer four times necessitates a good ending at the time of death,

أَسْتَغْفِرُ اللهَ الْعَظِيْمَ الَّذِيْ لَا إِلٰهَ إِلَّا هُوَ
الْحَيَ الْقَيُّومَ الَّذِيْ لَا يَمُوْتُ وَأَتُوبُ إِلَيْهِ رَبِّ اغْفِرْلِي

I seek the forgiveness of Allah, the Mighty, whom there is none other but He, the Living, the Self-Established, who does not perish, and I turn in repentance to Him, My Lord forgive me.

Some of the gnostics have said that whoever says after the Maghrib prayer before speaking to anyone, '*O Allah, send blessings and peace upon our liege lord Muḥammad ﷺ and upon his folk and his Companions as many as the number of letters that flow through the pen*' ten times will die upon faith.

اللهُمَ صَلِّ وَسَلِّمْ عَلَى خَاتِمِ الأَنْبِيَاءِ وَسَيِّدِ الأَصْفِيَاءِ وَمَعْدِنِ الأَسْرَارِ
وَمَنْبَعِ الأَنْوَارِ وَكَمَالِ الْكَوْنَيْنِ وَشَرَفِ الثَّقَلَيْنِ وَسَيِّدِ الدَّارَيْنِ المَخْصُوْصِ
بِقَابِ القَوْسَيْنِ سَيِّدِنَا مُحَمَّدٍ

O Allah, send blessings and peace upon the Seal of the Prophets, the Master of the Pure, the Mine of Secrets, the Spring of Lights, the Perfection of the Two Worlds, the Honour of the Two Creations[4]*, the Master of the Two Abodes, the Elect One of two bows' length*[5] *, our liege lord Muḥammad*$_2$ ﷺ

4 Literally 'the two heavy ones' referring to mankind and jinn, whose constitution is heavy, as opposed to angels whose constitution is light

5 A reference to the verse: '*Till he was at two bows' length, or nearer*' (53:8)

2 - THE PRAYER FOR HEALING[3]

اللهُمَّ صَلِّ عَلَى سَيِّدِنَا مُحَمَّدٍ طِبِّ القُلُوبِ وَدَوَائِهَا
وَعَافِيَةِ الأَبْدَانِ وَشِفَائِهَا* وَنُورِ الأَبصَارِ وَضِيَائِهَا وَعَلَى آلِهِ وَصَحبِهِ وَسَلِّم

O Allah, send blessings and peace upon our liege lord Muḥammad ﷺ, the medicine of hearts and their treatment, the soundness of bodies and their cure, the light of vision and its illumination, and [send blessings] upon his folk and his Companions.

This is a prayer of inward and outward healing which is read 2,000 times for any illness and it is said (that it can be read) 400 times. Reading this will be a cure by the permission of Allah the Exalted. It is recommended to add to this (after the asterisk above):

* وَقُوتِ الأَروَاحِ وَغَذَائِهَا

The sustenance of souls and their nourishment.

The eloquence and beauty of this addition is clear.

3 - THE PRAYER TO REMOVE WORRIES, GRIEF AND OTHER ILLNESSES[4]

اللهُمَ صَلِّ عَلَى سَيِّدِنَا مُحَمَّدٍ صَلَاةً تُحِلُّ بِهَا العُقَدَ وَتُفَرِّجُ بِهَا الكَربُ
وَتَنشَرِحُ بِهَا الصُدُورُ وَتُيَسِّرُ بِهَا الأُمُورُ وَعَلَى آلِهِ وَصَحبِهِ وَسَلِّم

O Allah, send blessings and peace upon our liege lord Muḥammad ﷺ a blessing which unties the knot, and by which afflictions are relieved, chests are expanded, affairs are lightened, and [send blessings] upon his folk and Companions.

4 - THE PRAYER TO ALLEVIATE GRIEF

اللهُمَّ صَلِّ وَسَلِّم وَبَارِك عَلَى سَيِّدِنَا مُحَمَّدٍ النَّبِي الأُمِّي
الحَبِيبِ المَحبُوبِ شَافِي العِلَلِ وَمُفَرِّجِ الكُرُوبِ وَعَلَى آلِهِ وَصَحْبِهِ وَسَلِّم

O Allah, send blessings and peace and beatify our liege lord Muḥammad ﷺ, the unlettered Prophet, the intensely beloved, the healer of sickness, the one who alleviates grief, and [send blessings] upon his folk and Companions.

5 - THE PRAYER FOR REMOVING DIFFICULTIES[5]

أَستَغفِرُ اللهَ العَظِيمَ مِن كُلِّ ذَنبٍ أَتَيتُهُ أَو هَمَمتُ بِهِ، يَا اللهُ يَا اللهُ يَا اللهُ صَلِّ عَلَى حَبِيبِكَ وَخَلِيلِكَ وَصَفِيِّكَ سَيِّدِنَا مُحَمَّدٍ وَآلِهِ وَصَحبِهِ وَسَلِّم وَاقضِ حَاجَتِي وَاقبَلْ دَعوَتِي وَعَجِّل لِي بِالإِجَابَةِ يَا أَرحَمَ الرَّاحِمِينَ، إِنَّكَ عَلَى كُلِّ شَيءٍ قَدِيرٌ وَبِالإِجَابَةِ جَدِيرٌ، آمِينَ آمِينَ آمِينَ

I seek forgiveness from Allah, the Mighty, from every sin that I have committed or those which I had intended. O Allah, O Allah, O Allah! Send blessings and peace upon Your beloved, Your intimate friend, Your pure being, our liege lord Muḥammad ﷺ, and upon his folk and Companions. Fulfil my needs and accept my supplication and hasten its answer, O Most Merciful of those who show mercy. You have absolute power over everything and You are most worthy of answering this prayer. Āmīn, Āmīn, Āmīn!

The author, Sayyid Abdullāh bin ʿAlawī bin Ḥusayn al-ʿAṭṭās, may Allah have mercy on him and forgive his sins and cover his faults, and author of the book, *The Way of the People of Guidance*, and who passed in the year 1334 AH said, 'Whoever wishes to have his difficulties removed, his faults covered, and his sins forgiven, and obtain everything he seeks should habituate himself upon the recital of this supplication. This should be read at least 100 times each day.'

اللهُمَّ صَلِّ عَلَى النُّورِ السَّاطِعِ الذَّاتِ الأَحَدِي، يَا مَدَدِي خُذ بِيَدِي
وَعَلَيكَ مُعتَمَدِي بِأَلفِ أَلفِ كٓهيعٓصٓ حمٓ عٓسٓقٓ، بُدُّوحٌ بُدُّوحٌ
وَعَلَى آلِهِ وَصَحْبِهِ وَسَلِّم

O Allah, send blessings and peace upon the radiant light, the unified essence, O source of assistance, take me by the hand, I depend on you by a million Kāf Hā Yā ʿAyn Ṣād, Ḥā Mīm ʿAyn Sīn Qāf. Buddūḥ[6]*, and [send blessings] upon his folk and Companions.*

Whoever has a need before Allah he sincerely wants to be fulfilled then he should sit facing the Qibla in a state of purity, directing himself towards Allah, the Exalted, with sincerity and say this prayer 100 times, and then ask Allah, the Exalted, regarding his need and it will be fulfilled by Allah's permission.

The following is read fourteen times in order to open the doors of ease:

6 A name or attribute of Allah from the Syriac with a similar meaning to *al-Wadūd* (the Loving)

اللهُمَّ صَلِّ وَسَلِّم عَلَى سَيِّدِنَا مُحَمَّدٍ صَلَاةَ العَبدِ الحَائِرِ المُحتَاجِ
الَّذِي ضَجَّ مِن ضِيقٍ وَحَرَجٍ فَالتِجَاءُ إِلَى بَابِ الكَرِيمِ

O Allah, send blessings and peace upon our liege lord Muḥammad ﷺ, the prayer of an erring needy slave who cries out due to constriction and difficulty and the refuge is to door of the Generous.[7]

اللَّهُمَّ صَلِّ عَلَى المَوصُوفِ بِالكَرَمِ وَالجُودِ

O Allah, send blessings upon the one who is characterised by generosity and munificence.

Whoever has a need before Allah should stand at night for two units of prayer with the intention of requesting goodness and should then send blessings upon the Prophet ﷺ using the aforementioned formula 1100 times.

اللهُمَّ بِحَقِّ سَيِّدِنَا مُحَمَّدٍ وَآلِ سَيِّدِنَا مُحَمَّدٍ صَلِّ عَلَى سَيِّدِنَا مُحَمَّدٍ وَآلِ سَيِّدِنَا
مُحَمَّدٍ وَاملأْ قَلْبِي وَصَدرِي بِمَحَبَّةِ سَيِّدِنَا مُحَمَّدٍ وَآلِ سَيِّدِنَا مُحَمَّدٍ وَاجعَلهَا
فَكَّاكًا لِي مِن الدَّينِ وَالهَمِّ وَعَلَى آلِهِ وَصَحبِهِ وَسَلِّم

O Allah, by the right of our liege lord Muḥammad ﷺ and the folk of our liege lord Muḥammad ﷺ, send blessings upon our liege lord Muḥammad ﷺ and upon his folk of our liege lord Muḥammad ﷺ, and fill my heart and chest with the love of our liege lord Muḥammad ﷺ and the folk of our liege lord Muḥammad ﷺ, and make this a liberator for me from debt and worry and [send blessings] upon his folk and Companions.

The *Sayyid*, the *Sharīf* al-Jifrī al-Makkī, may Allah lengthen his life said, 'This formula of praise came forth as a gift and a bounty to me from the Beloved ﷺ during a visit to the Rawḍah of the Prophet ﷺ'. The Sayyid was worried and had debts upon him and it was not long before Allah alleviated his worries and fulfilled the debt.

اللهُمَّ صَلِّ عَلَى سَيِّدِنَا مُحَمَّدٍ وَعَلَى أَهْلِ بَيْتِهِ يَا رَبِّ تَوَسَّلْتُ إِلَيْكَ
بِحَبِيبِكَ وَرَسُولِكَ وَعَظِيمِ القَدْرِ عِنْدَكَ سَيِّدِنَا مُحَمَّدٍ صَلَّى اللهُ عَلَيْهِ وَسَلَّمَ
فِي قَضَاءِ الحَاجَةِ الَّتِي أُرِيدُهَا

O Allah, send blessings upon our liege lord Muḥammad ﷺ and upon his
household. O my Lord, I seek your intercession by virtue of your Beloved,
your Messenger and by Your immense power, our liege lord Muḥammad ﷺ
to fulfil the need I wish [to be fulfilled].

The commentator narrated this prayer from Aḥmad b. Mūsā, from his father, from his grandfather in which he said, 'Whoever reads this 100 times each day, Allah will fulfil 100 of his needs of which 30 pertain to the worldly life.'

Ibn Ḥajar mentioned in *The Book of Thunderbolts* that he narrated from Jaʿfar ibn Muḥammad ibn Jābir *marfuʿan*[7], "Whoever sends blessings upon Muḥammad ﷺ and upon his household 100 times, Allah will fulfil 100 of his needs, 70 of which pertain to the life Hereafter".

Shaykh al-Sajāʿī mentioned this in his *Marginal Notes* with the wording: 'O Allah, send blessings and peace upon Muḥammad ﷺ and upon the folk of our liege lord Muḥammad ﷺ, and upon his household.'[8]

7 A ḥadīth which is attributed to the Prophet ﷺ

It is reported on the authority of Muʿādh ibn Jabal ﷺ that the Prophet ﷺ said to him, 'Shall I not teach you a supplication that were the like of *ṣabīr*[8] to be upon you in debt, Allah would fulfil it for you?'

﴿قُلِ ٱللَّهُمَّ مَٰلِكَ ٱلْمُلْكِ تُؤْتِى ٱلْمُلْكَ مَن تَشَآءُ وَتَنزِعُ ٱلْمُلْكَ مِمَّن تَشَآءُ
وَتُعِزُّ مَن تَشَآءُ وَتُذِلُّ مَن تَشَآءُ ۖ بِيَدِكَ ٱلْخَيْرُ ۖ إِنَّكَ عَلَىٰ كُلِّ شَىْءٍ قَدِيرٌ ﴿٢٦﴾
تُولِجُ ٱلَّيْلَ فِى ٱلنَّهَارِ وَتُولِجُ ٱلنَّهَارَ فِى ٱلَّيْلِ ۖ وَتُخْرِجُ ٱلْحَىَّ مِنَ ٱلْمَيِّتِ وَتُخْرِجُ
ٱلْمَيِّتَ مِنَ ٱلْحَىِّ ۖ وَتَرْزُقُ مَن تَشَآءُ بِغَيْرِ حِسَابٍ﴾

رَحْمٰنَ الدُّنيَا وَالآخِرَةِ وَرَحِيمَهُمَا تُعطِي مَن تَشَاءُ مِنهُمَا
وَتَمنَعُ مَن تَشَاءُ مِنهُمَا ، ارحَمنِي رَحمَةً تُغنِنِي بِهَا عَن رَحمَةِ مَن سِوَاكَ

8 Author's footnote: It is the name of a mountain in Yemen and is mentioned by al-Ṭabarānī in *al-Ṣaghīr*, by al-Ṣuyūṭī in *al-Durr al-Manthūr*, by al-Mundhirī in *al-Targhīb wa'l-Tarhīb*, and by ibn ʿAjība in *al-Baḥr al-Madīd*

Say: 'O Allah, Owner of Sovereignty! You bestow sovereignty on whom You will, and take away sovereignty from whom You will; You exalt whom You will and abase whom You will. In Your hand lies all that is good; You have power overall things. "You cause the night to pass into the day, and the day to pass into the night. You bring forth the living from the dead and the dead from the living; and You give sustenance to whom You choose, without stint.'

The Compassionate in the worldly life and in the Hereafter, and the Merciful in both, you give to whomever You will from the two worlds, and You withhold from whomever You will. Show me a mercy that renders me free of (asking for) mercy from anyone but You.

8 - THE PRAYER FOR PROSPERITY IN THE TWO WORLDS[9]

Whoever reads the following 100 times in morning and evening will prosper in the two worlds:

اللهُمَ صَلِّ عَلَى سَيِّدِنا مُحَمَّدٍ وَآلِهِ وَسَلِّم
اللهُمَ صَلِّ عَلَى سَيِّدِنَا مُحَمَّدٍ الفَاتِحِ لَمَا أُغلِق وَالخَاتَمِ لِمَا سَبَقَ نَاصِرِ الحَقِّ
بِالحَقِّ وَالهَادِي إِلَى صِرَاطِكَ المُستَقِيمِ وَعَلَى آلِهِ حَقَّ قَدرِهِ وَمِقدَارِهِ العَظِيمِ

O Allah, send blessings and peace upon our liege lord Muḥammad ﷺ and upon his folk and Companions. O Allah, send blessings upon our liege lord Muḥammad ﷺ, the opener to that which is closed, the seal of that which has preceded, the one who gives triumph to the truth by the Real, the guide unto Your upright path and [send blessings] upon his folk in accordance with His power and His immense measure.

9 - THE PRAYER UPON THE PROPHET ﷺ READ AT THE TIME OF HARVEST[10]

بِسمِ اللهِ الرَّحمٰنِ الرَّحِيمِ

﴿أَفَرَءَيْتُم مَّا تَحْرُثُونَ﴾

بَلِ اللهُ الزَّارِعُ وَالمُنبِتُ وَالمُبلِغُ، اللهُمَّ صَلِّ عَلَى سَيِّدِنَا مُحَمَّدٍ وَعَلَى آلِ
سَيِّدِنَا مُحَمَّدٍ وَارزُقنَا ثَمَرَهُ وَجَنِّبنَا ضَرَرَهُ وَاجعَلنَا لِأَنعُمِكَ مِن الشَّاكِرِينَ
[وَلِآلَائِكَ مِنَ الذَّاكِرِينَ وَبَارِك لَنَا فِيهِ يَا رَبَّ العَالَمِينَ]

In the name of Allah, the Compassionate, the Merciful
Have you seen that which you sow?[9]

Rather it is Allah who cultivates the land and causes crops to grow and causes outcomes. O Allah, send blessings upon our liege lord Muḥammad ﷺ and upon the folk of our liege lord Muḥammad ﷺ and bring us its produce and

9 al Wāqi'a (56:63)

distance us from its harm and make us from amongst the grateful through Your blessings [and from the mindful through Your favours, and bless us in this, O Lord of Creations][10].

Imam al-Qurtubī says in his commentary on the Qur'an,

> 'It is recommended for the one who sows seeds in the earth to read His saying, Exalted be He *Have you seen that which you sow?* followed by the above supplication.
>
> It is said that this verse protects crops from all types of harm including worms, locusts and other such creatures. We have heard this from trustworthy sources and it has been tested and found to be true.'

10 This addition is the completion of the prayer in question and is taken from Imam al-Qurṭubī's *tafsīr*, *Jāmiʿ Aḥkām al-Qur'ān*

10 - THE PRAYER FOR PROSPERITY[11]

اللهُمَّ صَلِّ عَلَى سَيِّدِنَا مُحَمَّدٍ النَّبِي الأُمِّي وَعَلَى آلِهِ وَصَحبِهِ وَسَلِّم تَسلِيمًا
صَلَاةً تُفَتِّحُ لَنَا بِهَا أَبوَابَ الرِّضَى وَالتَّيسِيرِ وَتُغَلِّقُ بِهَا عَنَّا أَبوَابَ الشَّرِّ
وَالتَّعسِيرِ أَنتَ الرَّبُّ المَولَى نِعمَ المَولَى وَ نِعمَ النَّصِيرُ

O Allah, send immense blessings and peace upon our liege lord Muḥammad ﷺ and upon his folk and Companions, blessings which open for us the doors of pleasure and ease and which close the doors of evil and hardship. You are the Nurturer, the Protector, a Great Protector indeed and a Source of assistance.

It is narrated from Shaykh Abū Abdullāh Muḥammad b. Aḥmad al-Yūsī al-Sanūsī, may Allah bestow mercy upon him, that he said, 'From the things which have proven to grant prosperity is the reading of this prayer, seven times in the morning and seven times in the evening.'

11 - THE LITANY OF HUSAYN ﵁

TO REMOVE POVERTY AND OTHER AFFLICTIONS

اللهُمَّ إِنِّي أَسأَلُكَ بِمَلَائِكَتِكَ وَمَعَاقِدِ عِزِّكَ وَسُكَّانِ سَمٰوَاتِكَ وَأَرضِكَ
وَأَنبِيَائكَ وَرُسُلِكَ أَن تَستَجِيبَ لِي فَقَد رَهِقَنِي مِن أَمرِي عُسرًا فَأَسأَلُكَ
أَن تُصَلِّيَ عَلَى سَيِّدِنَا مُحَمَّدٍ وَآلِ مُحَمَّدٍ وَأَن تَجعَلَ لِي يُسرًا

O Allah, verily I ask You by virtue of Your angels, and by the essence of Your honour, and by the denizens of Your Heavens and Earth, and by your Prophets and Messengers that You answer my prayer for difficulty has overcome my affair, so I thereby ask You to send blessings upon Muḥammad ﷺ and to make this easy for me.

Whoever habituates themselves to reading the Litany of Ḥusayn ﵁ after each of the five obligatory prayers, before saying anything else whilst remaining seated will find therein a secret. This is however on the condition that one has permission, granted by those qualified to do so. It is fine however for one to read this whenever he wants at the time of supplication and this does not require permission.

12 - A PRAYER TO OPEN THE PATHWAYS OF PROVISION[12]

اللهُمَ صَلِّ عَلَى سَيِّدِنَا مُحَمَّدٍ الفَاتِحِ لِلْأَرْزَاقِ اسْمُهُ وَالْمُتَلَأْلِئُ بِالْأَنْوَارِ
جِسْمُهُ وَالْمُشَعْشَعُ بِالْأَسْرَارِ رَسْمُهُ وَعَلَى آلِهِ الطَّيِّبِيْنَ الطَّاهِرِيْنَ وَسَلِّمْ
عَلَيْهِمْ أَجْمَعِيْنَ

O Allah, send blessings upon our liege lord Muḥammad, his name opens of pathways of provision, his body shines with light, intertwined secrets are his hallmark, and [send blessings] upon his pure and flawless folk.

13 - A PRAYER WHICH IS PROVEN TO QUICKLY BRING FORTH PROVISION

اللهُمَّ صَلِّ عَلَى سَيِّدِنَا مُحَمَّدٍ بنِ عَبدِاللهِ
القَائِمِ بِحُقُوقِ اللهِ مَا ضَاقَت إِلَّا وَفَرَّجَهَا اللهُ

O Allah, send blessings upon our liege lord Muḥammad ﷺ ibn Abdillah, the establisher of Divine rights; which had become constrained, except that Allah had caused it to open up.

This prayer is to be read 313 upto 1000 times.

It is read 313 times after the two unit Prayer of Need (*Ṣalāt al-Ḥāja*), after ʿIsha and in privacy with presence of heart, facing the Qibla, and one should not talk whilst invoking. This should be done for 7 or 11 days.

14 - THE PRAYER UPON THE PROPHET ﷺ FOR THE ONE WHO IS UNABLE TO SLEEP[13]

﴿إِنَّ ٱللَّهَ وَمَلَٰٓئِكَتَهُۥ يُصَلُّونَ عَلَى ٱلنَّبِيِّۚ
يَٰٓأَيُّهَا ٱلَّذِينَ ءَامَنُوا صَلُّوا عَلَيْهِ وَسَلِّمُوا تَسْلِيمًا﴾

Allah and His angels bless the Prophet. O you who believe! Bless him and salute him with a worthy salutation![11]

Ibn Bashkawāl mentioned on the authority of ʿAbd al-Quddūs al-Rāzī that he prescribed the person who is unable to sleep, to say, 'If you want to sleep, then read the verse [mentioned above].'

11 al Aḥzāb (33:56)

أَعُوذُ بِاللهِ مِنَ الشَّيطَانِ الرَّجِيمِ

بِسمِ اللهِ الرَّحمٰنِ الرَّحِيمِ

اللَّهُمَّ بِحَقِّ سَيِّدِنَا مُحَمَّدٍ أَرِنِي وَجهَ سَيِّدِنَا مُحَمَّدٍ حَالًا وَمَآلًا

I seek refuge in Allah from the accursed Devil (5 times)
In the name of Allah, the Compassionate, the Merciful (5 times)
By the right of our liege lord Muḥammad, allow me to see the face of our liege lord Muḥammad ﷺ in the present and in the future.

Shaykh Muḥammad Abu'l Mawāhib al-Shādhilī ﵁ said, 'I saw the Messenger of Allah ﷺ in a dream and he said to me, "When you go to sleep, say, 'I seek refuge in Allah five times, in the name of Allah,' five times and then say, 'By the right of our liege lord Muḥammad, allow me to see the face of our liege lord Muḥammad ﷺ in the present and in the future.' If you say this when sleeping, I shall indeed come to you and I will not fail to do so."'

The following prayer is read 313 times:

اللهُمَّ صَلِّ عَلَى سَيِّدِنَا مُحَمَّدٍ الجَامِعِ لِأَسرَارِكَ
وَالدَّالِّ عَلَيكَ وَعَلَى آلِهِ وَصَحْبِهِ وَسَلِّم

O Allah, send blessings and peace upon our liege lord Muḥammad ﷺ, the gatherer of Your secrets, the waymark to You, and [send blessings] upon his folk and his Companions.

اللهُمَّ حَبِّبْنِي إِلَى حَبِيبِكَ مُحَمَّدٍ سَيِّدِنَا مُحَمَّدٍ
صَلَّى اللهُ عَلَيهِ وَسَلَّمَ

O Allah, make me beloved to Your beloved ﷺ
our liege lord Muḥammad ﷺ

This prayer is read from a hundred to a thousand times. It has been mentioned that ibn ʿArabī had a daily litany of a thousand. My master, Shaykh Abu'l ʿAbbās al-Mursī ؓ said, 'From the daily litanies that I read is the following:

اللَّهُمَ حَبِّب نَبِيَّكَ مُحَمَّدًا صَلَّى اللهُ عَلَيهِ وَسَلَّمَ فِيَّ

O Allah, instil in me the love of your Prophet, Muḥammad ﷺ

A thousand times each night and I do so because I know that when he ﷺ loves me, he suffices me of the worries of worldly life and the Hereafter, by the assistance of Allah.'

So understand this and work in order to attach yourself to this and Allah, the Exalted will take the affair of your guidance upon Himself, and all praise is for Allah, the Nurturer of all creation.

اللهُمَّ صَلِّ وَسَلِّم وَبَارِك عَلَى سَيِّدِنَا مُحَمَّدٍ النَّبِي الأُمِّي الحَبِيبِ العَالِي القَدرِ العَظِيمِ الجَاهِ وَعَلَى آلِهِ وَصَحْبِهِ وَسَلِّم عَدَدَ مَا عَلِمتَ وَزِنَةَ مَا عَلِمتَ وَمِلءَ مَا عَلِمتَ

O Allah, send blessings and peace and beatify our liege lord Muḥammad ﷺ, the unlettered Prophet, the beloved, the exalted, the one of esteemed power, the great, the glorious, and upon his folk and Companions, in accordance with your knowledge, and with the adornment of your knowledge and with the fill of your knowledge.[16]

It is mentioned that this prayer removes the veils between the invoker and supremely beloved ﷺ. The least it should be recited is 10 times, and it is highly recommended to read it 100 times on the night of Friday[12].

12 *Laylat al-Jumu'ah* meaning Thursday night, since night precedes day.

17 - THE PRAYER OF AHMAD, THE MESSENGER OF ALLAH[17] ﷺ

سَيِّدُنَا مُحَمَّدٌ رَسُولُ اللهِ صَلَى اللهُ عَلَيهِ وَسَلَّم،
سَيِّدُنَا أَحْمَدُ رَسُولُ اللهِ صَلَى اللهُ عَلَيهِ وَسَلَّم

Our liege lord Muḥammad ﷺ is the Messenger of Allah, may Allah send blessings and peace upon him. Our liege lord Aḥmad ﷺ is the Messenger of Allah, may Allah send blessings and peace upon him.

From the unique qualities of this prayer is that whoever reads this prayer 35 times on the last Friday of Rajab whilst the *khaṭīb* is delivering his second sermon will not have his provisions cut off from him.

Al-Damīrī has mentioned in *The Life of Animals* in the section on speech with man, which has been transmitted from Shaykh Shihāb al-Dīn Aḥmad al-Būnī in his book *The Secret of Secrets*, 'Whoever writes on a piece of paper "Muḥammad, the Messenger of Allah, Aḥmad, the Messenger of Allah," thirty five times after the Friday prayer, whilst in a state of purity and carries it with him – Allah will strengthen him in obedience and assistance in gaining blessings. He will be protected from the whisperings of the demons, and if he perpetually looks at the piece of paper every day at sunrise, and he sends blessings upon Muḥammad ﷺ, then he will find in it a subtle secret, which has proven to be true.[18]

18 - A PRAYER FOR TEACHING STUDENTS

اللهُمَ صَلِّ وَسَلِّم عَلَى سَيِّدِنَا مُحَمَّدٍ مُحِيِي النُّفُوسِ
صَلَاةً تُسعِدُنَا بِهَا فِي جَمِيعِ الدُّرُوسِ وَعَلَى آلِهِ وَصَحبِهِ وَسلِّم

اللهُمَ اجعَل دَرسَنَا فِي كُلِّ عَامٍ أَوَّلَهُ صَلَاحًا وَأَوسَطَهُ فَلَاحًا وَآخِرَهُ نَجَاحًا

O Allah, send blessings and peace upon our liege lord Muḥammad ﷺ, the reviver of souls, a prayer by which we attain felicity in all of our classes, and [send blessings] upon his folk and Companions.

O Allah, in each year, make the former part of our lesson rectitude, the midst, success and the latter part salvation.

19 - A PRAYER THAT PROCURES OPENINGS IN KNOWLEDGE

اللَّهُمَ صَلِّ وَسَلِّم عَلَى سَيِّدِنَا مُحَمَّدٍ صَلَاةً تُخرِجُنِي بِهَا مِن ظُلُمَاتِ الوَهِمِ وَتُكرِمُنِي بِنُورِ الفَهمِ وَتُوضِحُ لِي مَا أَشكَلَ حَتَّى أَفهَمَ إِنَّكَ تَعلَمُ وَلَا أَعلَمُ وَأَنتَ عَلَّامُ الغُيُوبِ

O Allah, send blessings and peace upon our liege lord Muḥammad ﷺ, a blessing which removes me from the darkness of delusion, and which ennobles me with the light of comprehension, and which clarifies that which was unclear, so that I may understand that it is You alone who knows, and I know not, and You are most knowledgeable of the unseen.

20 - A PRAYER WHICH BEQUEATHS UNDERSTANDING[19]

بِسمِ اللهِ الرَّحمٰنِ الرَّحِيمِ
اللهُمَّ فَهِّمنِي عِلمَ الشَّرِيعَةِ وَالطَّرِيقَةِ وَالحَقِيقَةِ وَاستَعمِلنِي بِهَا
بِحَقِّ سَيِّدِنَا مُحَمَّدٍ صَلّى اللهُ عَلَيهِ وَسَلَّمَ وَآلِهِ وَصَحبِهِ أَجمَعِينَ

In the name of Allah, the Compassionate, the Merciful, give me understanding and the teach me the Sacred Law, the Spiritual Way and Realisation, and make use of me by it by virtue of our liege lord Muḥammad ﷺ and his folk and Companions.

The above should be written should be written on the inside of a cup [with soluble ink] and then pour in the water so that the ink dissolves and then drunk.

21 - PRAYERS WHOSE BENEFITS ARE IMMENSE

اللَّهُمَّ صَلِّ عَلَى سَيِّدِنَا وَنَبِيِّنَا وَمَولَانَا مُحَمَّدٍ وَعَلَى آلِ سَيِّدِنَا مُحَمَّدٍ صَلَاةً تُقَيِّدُنَا بِهَا يَا جَبَّارُ إِلَى طَرِيقِ الخَيرَاتِ وَمِن الهَمِّ وَالغَمِّ وَالفَرَجِ

O Allah, send blessings upon our liege lord and Prophet and protector Muḥammad ﷺ and upon the folk of our liege lord Muḥammad ﷺ, a blessing which leads us to the way of goodness and away from worry, grief and distress, O Compeller.

Whoever reads this twice every day, Allah will rid from him demonic insinuations in every act of worship and the devil will be unable to ruin any of his acts of worship, and he will not be disturbed during worship.

اللَّهُمَّ صَلِّ عَلَى سَيِّدِنَا وَنَبِيِّنَا وَمَولَانَا مُحَمَّدٍ وَعَلَى آلِ سَيِّدِنَا مُحَمَّدٍ صَلَاةً
تَستَجلِبُ لَنَا بِهَا يَا مُصَوِّرُ رِضَاكَ يُطَهِّرُنَا مِنَ الأَدْنَاسِ وَالوَسَخِ

O Allah, send blessing upon our liege lord and Prophet and protector Muḥammad ﷺ and upon the folk of our liege lord Muḥammad ﷺ, a blessing which thereby seeks your pleasure, and which cleanses us from impurity and filth, O Fashioner.

Whoever is habitual upon this prayer, openings will approach him. Allah will ease for him the difficulties of worship and Allah will send to him someone who rectifies his state and Allah will protect him from doubt and delusions when he is alone.

اللَّهُمَّ صَلِّ عَلَى سَيِّدِنَا وَنَبِيِّنَا وَمَولَانَا مُحَمَّدٍ وَعَلَى آلِ سَيِّدِنَا مُحَمَّدٍ
صَلَاةً تُعِينُنَا بِهَا يَا قَوِيُّ عَلَى مَحَبَّتِهِ وَتَعظِيمِهِ مِنَ الآنِ إِلَى الأَبَدِ

O Allah, send blessing upon our liege lord and Prophet and protector Muḥammad ﷺ and upon the folk of our liege lord Muḥammad ﷺ, a blessing which assists us in loving and venerating him ﷺ from now and for eternity, O Powerful!

This prayer procures the pleasure and love of the people of goodness, such as the shaykhs.

This is read 66 times and whoever reads it 1000 times, Allah will prevent the person from acts of disobedience. Likewise, Allah will prevent any matter affecting his righteous actions, and the love of our liege lord Muḥammad ﷺ will become firmly established within him.

22 - A PRAYER TO BE READ AFTER THE FIVE DAILY PRAYERS[20]

It is narrated on the authority of Abū Umāmah ؓ from the Prophet ﷺ that he said, 'Whoever supplicates with these prayers at the end of each obligatory prayer, my intercession is due for him on the Day of Rising:'

اللَّهُمَّ آتِ سَيِّدَنَا مُحَمَّدًا الوَسِيلَةَ وَاجعَل
فِي المُصطَفَينِ مَحَبَّتَهُ وَفِي العَالِينَ دَرَجَتَهُ وَفِي المُقَرَّبِينَ دَارَه

O Allah, bestow upon our liege lord Muḥammad ﷺ the wasīlah[13] *and place his love within the chosen ones, and in the lofty ranks his rank and in the proximate ones his abode.*

---

13 On the authority of ʿAbdullah b. ʿAmr al-ʿĀṣ ؓ, he heard the Messenger of Allah ﷺ say, "When you hear the call [to prayer], then say as the [*mu'adhdhin*] says. Then send blessings upon me and whoever sends a single blessing upon me, Allah will send ten blessings upon him. Then ask Allah that I attain *al-wasīlah* - a rank in Paradise which is only for one of the slaves of Allah, and I hope that it will be me. So whoever asks that I attain it, my intercession will become available for him"' (*Muslim*)

23 - A PRAYER TO BE READ AFTER THE FAJR AND MAGHRIB PRAYERS

﴿إِنَّ ٱللَّهَ وَمَلَٰٓئِكَتَهُۥ يُصَلُّونَ عَلَى ٱلنَّبِيِّۚ
يَٰٓأَيُّهَا ٱلَّذِينَ ءَامَنُوا۟ صَلُّوا۟ عَلَيْهِ وَسَلِّمُوا۟ تَسْلِيمًا﴾

اللَّهُمَّ صَلِّ عَلَيهِ

Allah and His angels bless the Prophet. O you who believe! Bless him and salute him with a worthy salutation![14]

O Allah, send blessings upon him ﷺ (100 times)

On the authority of Jābir ﷺ, 'The Messenger of Allah ﷺ said, "Whoever sends blessings upon me 100 times when he prays the dawn prayer before speaking, Allah, the Exalted, will fulfil 100 needs for him, 30 of which will relate to the temporal life and 70 needs relate to the Hereafter. And so too for the evening prayer," And they said, 'How does one send blessings upon you, O Messenger of Allah?' and he said,

14 al-Aḥzāb (33:56)

“*Allah and His angels bless the Prophet. O you who believe! Bless him and salute him with a worthy salutation!* O Allah, send blessings upon him ﷺ until it numbers 100.”[21]

The *sayyid* and scholar of hadith, Imam Muḥammad bin ‘Alī Khard mentioned in some of his works, with an unbroken chain to the Prophet ﷺ that: ‘Whoever reads [the aforementioned verse] after the dawn and evening prayer, and then reads O Allah, send blessings upon him 100 times, Allah will fulfil 100 of his needs – 30 in the worldly life and 70 in the Hereafter.’

It is called the Prayer of the Heart (*al-ḍamīr*), and it is befitting for the sincere wayfarer to habituate himself upon this. We have seen many of the righteous reciting this immediately after the prayer before speaking to anyone.[22]

24 - THE PRAYER OF THE ONE OF IMMENSE POWER ﷺ

اللَّهُمَّ صَلِّ عَلَى سَيِّدِنَا مُحَمَّدٍ النَّبِيِّ الأُمِّيِّ الحَبِيبِ
العَالِي القَدرِ العَظِيمِ الجَاهِ وَعَلَى آلِهِ وَصَحبِهِ وَسَلِّم

O Allah, send blessings and peace upon our liege lord Muḥammad, the unlettered prophet, the beloved one of immense power, the one of tremendous glory, and [send blessings] upon his folk and his companions.

This is the prayer of immense power (*ʿālī al-qadr*). Shaykh al-Ṣāwī transmitted to us in his commentary on *Salawat al-Dardīr*, and ʿAllāma Muḥammad al-Amir al-Ṣaghīr in his *Thabāt* from Imam al-Suyūṭī that whoever is consistent upon this prayer, every Friday night[15], even it just be once, he will be buried in his grave by the Prophet ﷺ.

Sayyid Aḥmad Daḥlān mentioned the benefits of this prayer in his collection, 'And from the virtuous formulas of praise which have been mentioned by a great number of gnostics is that whoever is continuous upon reading this on

15 *Laylat al-jumuʿah* meaning Thursday night

the night of Friday, be it just once, the form of the soul of the Prophet ﷺ will be unveiled to the invoker's soul at the time of death, and at the time of his burial such that he will see that it is the Prophet ﷺ who is burying him.'

Some of the gnostics have also said, 'It is befitting for the one who is consistent upon this to read it 10 times every night and 100 times on the night of Friday so that by virtue of this bounty and goodness, he attains this great good, if Allah so wishes.[23]

And may Allah send peace and blessings upon our liege lord and protector Muḥammad and upon the folk and the companions of our liege lord and protector Muḥammad and praise is for Allah, the Lord of the worlds.

Appendix: The meaning of *ṣalāt*[16]

Imām al-Bukhārī mentions in his sound compendium that Abu'l-ʿĀliya said: The *ṣalāt* of Allah is His praise upon him ﷺ amongst the angels, and the *ṣalāt* of the angels is supplication for him. Ibn ʿAbbās ؓ said *yuṣallūna* means they send blessings.

Al-Ḥāfiẓ [ibn Ḥajr al-ʿAsqālanī] mentions in *Fatḥ al-Bārī*: According to ibn Abi Ḥātim on the authority of Muqātil ibn Ḥayyān,'The *ṣalāt* of Allah is His forgiveness and the *ṣalāt* of the angels is their seeking forgiveness.'

On the authority of ibn ʿAbbās, the meaning of *ṣalāt* of Allah is mercy and the *ṣalāt* of angels is seeking forgiveness. Al-Daḥḥāk b. Muzāhim said that the *ṣalāt* of Allah is mercy, and in another narration from him, His forgiveness, and the *ṣalāt* of angels is supplication.

Al-Ḥāfiẓ then said, 'The most correct of positions is that of Abu'l-ʿĀliya, that the meaning of the *ṣalāt* of Allah upon His Prophet ﷺ is His praise of him ﷺ and His venerating him. The *ṣalāt* of the angels and other than them is seeking this

---

16 This section is taken from *al-Ṣalāt ʿalā al-Nabī* ﷺ by Shaykh ʿAbdullāh Sirāj al-Dīn ؓ.

for him ﷺ from Allah. The meaning of this is seeking increase, not seeking *ṣalāt* itself.

The *ṣalāt* of Allah upon His noble Prophet ﷺ is perpetual and continual and does not cease. The evidence for this is Allah's saying, 'Verily Allah and His angels send *ṣalāt* upon the Prophet,'[17] as Allah, Exalted be He, is continually sending blessings upon His Prophet and beloved, and regarding the *ṣalāt* of angels and other creatures, it is seeking increase in this [for him ﷺ].

Undoubtedly, everything which has been mentioned by the scholars of the early generations ﷺ regarding the meanings of the *ṣalāt* of Allah upon His Prophet ﷺ are both true and correct, and there is no contradiction between the varying positions, as all of these positions mention aspects of the meaning of *ṣalāt* upon the beloved ﷺ.

This is because the *ṣalāt* of the Lord of Creation includes the meanings of praise, veneration, and ennoblement, and of elect affection, and elect mercy and elect forgiveness, and the like of that which pertains to the comprehensive meanings of goodness, virtue and honour, and of righteousness, praise and laud, light and illumination.

---

17 The verb used in the verse is in the present-future, which the scholars of Arabic grammar say denotes a continuous action.

The *ṣalāt* of the Lord of the Worlds in relation to His creation is elite (*khāṣṣa*), or of supreme election (*khāṣṣat al-khāṣṣa*), or general (*ʿāmma*) in nature. His *ṣalāt* upon the prophets is elite, in accordance with the rank of their prophecy and His *ṣalāt* is likewise elite for the people of proximity (*al-muqarrabīn*) and His saints in accordance with their ranks. His *ṣalāt* upon His most honourable beloved one, the Leader and Seal of the Prophets and Emissaries is of supreme election, in accordance with his supreme rank ﷺ. His *ṣalāt* upon the masses from the believers is general and in accordance with their faith.

He is the One who sends blessings upon you, as do His angels, in order to bring you from darkness to light, and He is merciful to the believers[18].

---

18 al-Aḥzāb (33:43)

Transliteration key

ا	a	ز	z	ق	q		
ب	b	س	s	ك	k		
ت	t	ش	sh	ل	l	ـَا	ā
ث	th	ص	ṣ	م	m	ـِي	ī
ج	j	ض	ḍ	ن	n	ـُو	ū
ح	ḥ	ط	ṭ	و	w		
خ	kh	ظ	ẓ	ه	h		
د	d	ع	ʿ	ي	y		
ذ	dh	غ	gh	ء	ʾ		
ر	r	ف	f				

Transliteration of prayers

1. *Allāhumma ṣalli ʿalā Sayyidinā Muḥammadin wa ʿalā ālihī wa ṣaḥbiḥī wa sallim bi ʿadadi kulli ḥarfin jarā bihil qalam*

   Astaghfirullāh al- ʿaẓīm alladhī lā ilāha illa hū al-Ḥayy al-Qayyūm alladhī la yamūtu wa atūbu ilayhī rabbigh firlī

   Allāhumma ṣalli wa sallim ʿalā khātamil ambiyā, wa sayyidil aṣfiyā wa maʿdīnil asrāri wa manbaʿil anwāri, wa kamāl al-kawnayn ﷺ wa sharaf ath thaqalayn wa sayyidid dārayn al-makhṣūṣi bi qābil qawsayni Sayyidinā Muḥammadin

2. *Allāhumma ṣalli ʿalā Sayyidinā Muḥammadin ṭibbil qulūbi wa dawā'ihā wa ʿāfiyatil abdāni wa shifā'ihā wa nūril abṣāri wa ḍiyā'ihā (wa qūtil arwāḥi wa ghadhā'ihā) wa ʿalā ālihī wa ṣaḥbiḥī wa sallim*

3. *Allāhumma ṣalli ʿalā Sayyidinā Muḥammadin ṣalātan tuḥillu bihal ʿuqda wa tufarriju bihal karbu wa tansharihu bihaṣ ṣudūru wa tuyassiru bihal umūru wa ʿalā ālihī wa ṣaḥbihī wa sallim*

4. *Allāhumma ṣalli wa sallim wa bārik ʿalā Sayyidina Muḥammadin annabiyyil ummī, al ḥabībil maḥbūb, shāfiyal ʿilali wa mufarrijil kurūbu wa ʿalā ālihī wa ṣaḥbihī wa sallim*

5. *Astghfirullāh al ʿaẓīm min kulli dhambin ātaytuhū aw hammamtu bi. Yā Allāh, yā Allāh, yā Allāh ṣalli ʿalā ḥabībika wa khalīlika wa ṣafiyyika Sayyidinā Muḥammadin wa ālihī wa ṣaḥbihī wa sallim waqḍi ḥājatī wa aqbil daʿwatī wa ʿajjil lī bil ijābati ya arḥam arraḥimīn. Innaka ʿala kulli shay'in qadīr wa bil ijābati jadīr. Āmīn, āmīn, āmīn.*

6. *Allāhumma ṣalli ʿalan nūris sāṭiʿadh dhātil ahadī. Ya madadi khudh bi yadī wa ʿalayka muʿtamadī bi aldi Kāf Hā Yā ʿAyn Ṣād. Buddūḥun Buddūḥun wa ʿalā ālihī wa ṣaḥbihī wa sallim*

   Allāhumma ṣalli wa sallim ʿalā Sayyidinā Muḥammadin ṣalātal ʿabdil ḥā'iri almuḥtājil ladhī dajja min ḍīqin wa ḥarajin faltijā'u ila bābil Karīm

   Allāhumma ṣalli ʿalal mawṣūfi bilkarami wal jūd

   Allāhumma biḥaqqi Sayyidinā Muḥammadin wa āli Sayyidinā Muḥammadin ṣalli ʿalā Sayyidinā Muḥammadin wa āli Sayyidinā Muḥammadin wamla' qalbī wa ṣadrī bi maḥabbati Sayyidinā Muḥammadin wa āli Sayyidinā Muḥammadin waj ʿalha fukkākan lī min addayni wal hamma wa ʿalā ālihī wa ṣaḥbihī wa sallim.

Allāhumma ṣalli ʿalā Sayyidinā Muḥammadin wa ʿalā āli baytihī yā Rabbi tawassaltu ilayka bi ḥabībika wa rusulika wa aẓīmil qadri ʿindaka Sayyidinā Muḥammadin ṣallAllāhu ʿalayhi wa sallama fī qaḍā ilḥājāt illati ūrīduhā.

7. Qulillāhumma mālikal mulki tuʿtil mulka man tashā'u wa tanziʿul mulka mimman tashā'u wa tuʿizzu man tashā'u wa tudhillu man tashā'u biyadikal khayr. Innaka ʿalā kulli shay'in qadīr. Tūlijul layla fin nahāri wa tūlijun nahāri fil layl wa tukhrijul ḥayya minal mayyiti wa tukhrijul mayyita min al ḥayyi wa tarzuqu man tashā'u bighayri ḥisāb.

Raḥmānud dunyā wal ākhirati wa raḥīmu humā tuʿtī man tashā'u min humā wa tamnaʿu tashā'u min humā. Irḥamnī raḥmatan tughninī bihā ʿan rahmatin min siwāk

8. Allāhumma ṣalli ʿalā Sayyidinā Muḥammadin wa ālihī wa ṣallim. Allāhumma ṣalli ʿalā Sayyidinā Muḥammadin al fātiḥi limā ughlaq wal khātama limā sabaqa, nāṣiril ḥaqqi bilḥaqqi wal hādi ila ṣirāṭikal mustaqīmi wa ʿalā ālihī ḥaqqa qadarihī wa miqdārihil ʿaẓīm

9. Bismillā hirraḥmān nirraḥīm, afara aytum mā taḥruthūn
Allāhumma ṣalli ʿalā Sayyidinā Muḥammadin wa āli Sayyidinā Muḥammadin warzuqnā thamaratan wa jannibnā ḍararahū wajʿalnā li'anʿumika minash shakirīn wa li ālā'ika minadh dhākirīn wa bārik lanā fīhi yā rabbal ʿālamīn

10. *Allāhumma ṣalli ʿalā Sayyidinā Muḥammadin annabiyyil ummi wa ʿalā ālihī wa ṣaḥbihī wa sallim taslimā ṣalātan tufattiḥu lanā bihā abwābar riḍā wat taysīri wa tughalliqu bihā ʿanna abwābash sharri wat taʿsiri antar rabbul mawlā wa niʿman naṣīr*

11. *Allāhumma innī as'aluka bi malā'ikatika wa muʿāqidi ʿizzika wa sukkāni samāwātika wa arḍika wa ambiyā'ika wa rusulika an tastajība lī fa qad raḥiqani min amri ʿusrā fa as'aluka an tuṣallia ʿalā Sayyidinā Muḥammadin wa an tajʿala lī yusrā*

12. *Allāhumma ṣalli ʿalā Sayyidinā Muḥammadin al fātiḥi lil arzāqi ismuhū mutalali'u bil anwāri jismuhū wal mushaʿshaʿu bil asrāri rasmuhū wa ʿalā ālihī ṭayyibīna aṭ ṭāhirīna wa sallim ʿalayhim ajamʿīn*

13. *Allāhumma ṣalli ʿalā Sayyidinā Muḥammadin ibni ʿAbdillāhi al qā'imi bi ḥuqūqillāhi mā ḍāqat illa wa farrajaha Allah.*

14. *InnAllāha wa malā'ikatahū yuṣallūna ʿalan nabī. Yā ayyuhal ladhīna āmanū ṣallū ʿalayhi wa sallimū taslīmā*

15. *Aʿūdhu billāhi minash shayṭan nirrajīm, Bismillā hirraḥmān nirraḥīm. Allāhumma biḥaqqi Sayyidinā Muḥammadin arinī wajha Sayyidinā Muḥammadin ḥālan wa mā'alan*

Allāhumma ṣalli ʿalā Sayyidinā Muḥammadin al jamīʿi li asrārika wad dālli ʿalayka wa ʿalā ālihī wa ṣaḥbihī wa sallim

16. *Allāhumma ḥabibnī ilā ḥabībika Muḥammadin Sayyidinā Muḥammadin ṣallAllāhu ʿalayhi wa sallam*

Allāhumma ḥabbib nabiyyaka Muḥammdan ṣallAllāhu ʿalayhi wa sallama fiyya

Allāhumma ṣalli wa sallim wa bārik ʿalā Sayyidinā Muḥammadin annabiyyil ummī, al ḥabībil ʿāliyil qadr, al ʿaẓīmil jāhi wa ʿalā ālihī wa ṣaḥbihī wa sallim ʿadada mā ʿalimta wa zinata mā ʿalimta wa mil'a mā ʿalimta

17. *Sayyidunā Muḥammadun rasūlullāhi ṣallAllāhu ʿalayhi wa sallim. Sayyidunā Aḥmad rasūlullāhi ṣallAllāhu ʿalayhi wa sallim.*

18. *Allāhumma ṣalli wa sallim ʿalā Sayyidinā Muḥammadin muḥyin nufūsi ṣalātan tusʿidunā bihā fi jamīʿid durūsi wa ʿalā ālihī wa ṣaḥbihī wa sallim.*

Allāhumma'jʿal darsanā fi kulli ʿāmin awwalahū ṣalāhan wa awsaṭahū falāḥan wa akhiruhū najāḥan.

19. *Allāhumma ṣalli ʿalā Sayyidinā Muḥammadin ṣalātanā tukhrijunī bihā min ẓulumātil wahmi wa tukrimunī bi nūril fahmi wa tuḍīhu lī mā ashkala ḥattā afhamu innaka taʿlamu wa la aʿlamu wa anta ʿallāmul ghuyūb*

20. Bisimillāhir raḥmānir raḥīm. Allāhumma fahhimnī ʿilmash sharīʿati wat ṭarīqati wal ḥaqīqati wastaʿmilnī bihā biḥaqqi Sayyidinā Muḥammadin ṣallAllāhu ʿalayhi wa sallama wa ālihī wa ṣaḥbibī ajmaʿīn

21. Allāhumma ṣalli ʿalā sayyidinā wa ḥabībinā wa mawlānā Muḥammadin wa ʿāla āli Sayyidinā Muḥammadin ṣalātan tuqayyidunā bihā yā Jabbāru ilā ṭarīqil khayrāti wa minal hammi wa ghammi wal faraji

Allāhumma ṣalli ʿalā sayyidinā wa ḥabībinā wa mawlānā Muḥammadin wa ʿalā āli Sayyidinā Muḥammadin ṣalātan tastajlibu lanā bihā yā Musawwiru riḍāka yaṭ'haruna minal adnāsi wal wasakh

Allāhumma ṣalli ʿalā sayyidinā wa ḥabībinā wa mawlānā Muḥammadin wa ʿalā āli Sayyidinā Muḥammadin ṣalātan tuʿīnunā bihā yā Qawiyyu ʿalā maḥabbatihī wa taʿẓīmihi minal āna ilal abad

22. Allāhumma āti Sayyidanā Muḥammadanil wasīlata wajʿal fil muṣṭafayni maḥabbatahu wa fil ʿālīna darajathu wa fil muqarrabīna dārahu

23. InnAllaha wa malā'ikatahū yuṣallūna ʿalan nabī. Yā ayyuhal ladhīna āmanū ṣallū ʿalayhi wa sallimū taslīmā
Allāhumma ṣalli ʿalayhi

24. *Allāhumma salli ʿalā Sayyidinā Muḥammadin annabī al ummī alḥabībil ʿāliyil qadril ʿaẓīmil jāhi wa ʿalā ālihī wa ṣaḥbihī wa sallim*

References

References in the text are made using superscript₁

1. Masālik al-Ḥunafā ilā Mashāriʿ al-Ṣalāt ʿalā al-Nabī al-Muṣtafā
2. al-Fawā'id wa al-Farā'id
3. Saʿādat al-Dārayn fī al-Ṣalāt ʿalā Sayyid al-Kawnayn
4. al-Fawā'id wa al-Farā'id
5. Fatḥ al-Rasūl wa Miftāḥ Bābihi li al-Dukhūl
6. Ghāyat al-Amānī
7. al-Fawā'id wa al-Farā'id
8. Afḍal al-Ṣalawāt ʿalā Sayyid al-Sādāt
9. Ghāyat al-Amānī
10. Masālik al-Ḥunafā ilā Mashāriʿ al-Ṣalāt ʿalā al-Nabī al-Muṣtafā
    Jāmiʿ Aḥkām al-Qur'ān
11. al-Safīnah al-Qādariyya
12. Khazīnah al-Ṣalawāt ʿalā Sayyid al-Kā'ināt
13. Masālik al-Ḥunafā ilā Mashāriʿ al-Ṣalāt ʿalā al-Nabī al-Muṣtafā

14. al-Ṭabaqāt al-Kubrā
15. ʿAmal al-Yawm wa al-Laylah
16. al-Minan al-Kubrā
17. al-Fawā'id wa al-Farā'id
18. Kayfiyyah al-Wuṣūl li Ru'yat Sayyidinā al-Rasūl
19. Saʿādat al-Dārayn fi al-Ṣalāt ʿalā Sayyid al-Kawnayn
20. al-Qawl al-Badīʿ fi al-Ṣalāt ʿalā al-Ḥabīb al-Shafiʿ
    al-Durr al-Manḍūd fi al-Ṣalāt wa al-Salām ʿalā Ṣāḥib al-Maqām al-Maḥmūd
21. Masālik al-Ḥunafā ilā Mashāriʿ al-Ṣalāt ʿalā al-Nabī al-Muṣtafā
22. al-Tadhkīr al-Muṣṭafā
23. Afḍal al-Ṣalawāt ʿalā Sayyid al-Sādāt
    Sharḥ al-Ṣalawāt al-Dardīr